Heart Of The Matter

Navigating life's ups and downs

Devika Anand

Copyright © Devika Anand
All Rights Reserved.

This book has been self-published with all reasonable efforts taken to make the material error-free by the author. No part of this book shall be used, reproduced in any manner whatsoever without written permission from the author, except in the case of brief quotations embodied in critical articles and reviews.

The Author of this book is solely responsible and liable for its content including but not limited to the views, representations, descriptions, statements, information, opinions, and references ["Content"]. The Content of this book shall not constitute or be construed or deemed to reflect the opinion or expression of the Publisher or Editor. Neither the Publisher nor Editor endorse or approve the Content of this book or guarantee the reliability, accuracy, or completeness of the Content published herein and do not make any representations or warranties of any kind, express or implied, including but not limited to the implied warranties of merchantability, fitness for a particular purpose.

The Publisher and Editor shall not be liable whatsoever...

Made with ❤ on the BookLeaf Publishing Platform
www.bookleafpub.in
www.bookleafpub.com

Dedication

"This book is dedicated to my daughter,Kanupriya,and my mother, Tanuja,who have been source of inspiration and love.Thank you for being the two pillars of my strength."

Preface

Welcome to Heart of the Matter, a collection of my poems that I am privileged to share with you. As an author, it is my first book,poured with heart and soul. My inspiration for the poems is life itself and the wonders of mother nature. I invite you to explore complexities of life through these poems,from the darkest agony to addressing challenges with hope and positivity.I hope these poems resonate with you and revitalize your soul.

Acknowledgements

"I would extend a heartfelt gratitude to everyone who supported and inspired me during my journey as a poet. I would especially like to thank my mother and daughter, who believed in my abilities and are a constant source of my inspiration. I have also drawn inspiration from life, Mother Nature, and my dear friends.I would like to thank BookLeaf Publishing for constant motivation."

1. Emotions must pass

Emotions must pass,don't keep them in heart,
 When the world is temporary ,then emotions must
depart

The feelings of love with faces of smile,
Joy to the world, we are all here for a while

Heart is no home for the feeling of pain,
Sadness do no good, loss is more & no gain

Fear is a emotion that slowly whispers,
Day and night no Joy as it quivers

Anxiety with its strength,comes for free,
Then refuses to disperse in you and me

Whatever you may feel, don't give up on love,
Purpose of living and gratitude above

But address all emotions as lost and found,
As they sink deep, without a sound

Emotions must pass,don't keep them in heart,
With the world is temporary ,then emotions must depart

2. Joy to the world

Joy is a feeling gifted with bliss
By the heavens about as a childhood kiss
When needs are less,just comfort of a toy
Wonders of innocence, baby dreams of joy

And connection with the nature has a lasting thrill
That surpasses ages and mountains that fulfill
Joy is felt in running down the stream
When moments are captured as delightful dreams
Joy is received in simple pleasures to cheer
Comforting our lives year after year
But if your wants are way to high
You only mourn with grief wherever you fly

Find the joy even in a flake of snow
And live your life in a natural flow
Joy is a feeling gifted with bliss
By the heavens above as a childhood bliss

3. Echoes of the heart

A feeling that transcends time and ages is love,
Which makes the sun shines in the sky above
Universal feeling that touches every heart,
And resonates in one self, together or apart
That spreads beyond the expanse of sea,
And gives eternal peace to you and me

It is beyond worldly pleasure of caresses and touch,
Where connections are deep and fondness is much
Which resides in us beyond times,forever,
Whether heaven or earth,binding us together

But if your passion is as dreadful as fire,
You are way to low in the hearth of desire
Never miss the pious longing in the eyes of a dove,
A tender feeling of delight in the world of love
A feeling that transcends times and ages is love,
Which makes the sun shines in the sky above

4. The Envy's Shadow

I am the emotion of envy and I have no shame,
Will burn you to hell in the fires of flame

They say I compare and my color is green,
No birth no dead I hardly can be seen

I am felt in every heart which pores with hate,
You cannot hide me in this mindless state'

I am a monster and I have a green eye,
I steal away your peace and you know why?

I am your insecurity were darkness falls,
Giving you sleepless nights as envy calls

I make you inhuman as I am the envy,
The heart sinks and shrinks making breath heavy

I am emotion of envy and I have no shame,
Will burn you to hell in the fires of flame

5. Fear's Icy Grip

I am a storm in a dreadful night that's called fear,
You may shake but can't escape as no road is clear

You may feel chilling dread that seeps in as cold,
Life becomes a mystery and haunted; wise people told

I am fog of uncertainty that spreads in the gloom,
And if you fail to overpower me, you are sure to doom

I am a dark mirror that will join you like a shadow,
And haunts your every step ;have my presents to follow

If you overcome me, I can't grow your sorrow,
You will restore your happiness, peace and no one to
borrow

I am a storm in a dreadful night that's called fear,
You make shake but can't escape as no road is clear

6. Heart' s Lullaby

My mind wanders and races without any rest,
Heart needs tranquil, solace is the best

Mind asks and demands in a commanding voice,
But listen to your heart and what is its choice

My mind blows in comparison and contrast asking for a
kickstart,
My heart calms me in serenity ,asking not to go fast

What is left when sadness overpowers and anxiety
remains,
Find space and slow down for peace to sustain

Where will you go with a broken heart and worn out
soul,
Heal and mend your heart to see it in it's best role

In the cracks of the heart,light will surely seep,
Guiding you forward where both love and peace meet

My heart wanders and races without any rest,
Heart needs tranquil ,solace is the best

7. Reminiscence

Recollection of laughter ,recollection of tears,
Memories of my childhood take away all my fear

Running down the hill ,walking along the stream was
such a joy,
I still reminisce the flute played by the Himalayan boy'

Walking behind the flocks ,running along the meadow
was my favorite play,
Relentlessly walking through the orchards to find my
beautiful way

The fragrance of blossom and rustle of leaf,
Those were undoubtedly the days of self discovery and
self belief

Moments of tranquil, moments of bliss are now so far
away,
Remembering those days and nights in my every pray

Recollection of laughter, recollection of tears,
Memories of my childhood take away all my fear

8. Acceptance

Acceptance is a state of mind that drives away denial,
It is about letting go things which are here for a while

It is the happiness of autumn tree to let go its dried leaf,
In the world of impermanence, don't waste the time in grief

It is the path that is wise and the path that is divine,
Don't regret for change, here nothing is mine

Weather acceptance of hardship in love or in work,
Don't hurt yourself with a burden of expectations, give your mind some comfort

Acceptance is a healing touch for life, fast or slow,
It brings us all to the same phase without any low

So ,in the world of impermanence maybe right or you maybe wrong,
Hug yourself the tightest ,as you can only sing your song

9. Beyond The Thorns

My life was about breaking the chain,
Keeping in my heart that was so insane

A marriage that suffocated beyond the depth of soul,
A life that I lived lonely with wife as my role

A life that was so painful, a life that was so dark,
For long I forgot that within me prevails some spark

For years I wore mask of happiness, a disguise to hide
my pain,
Had come to terms with life, without any purpose or
gain

Then decided to reclaim my freedom, it was a decision so
bold,
I left the man to hell who was so harsh and cold

The memories still lingered, I have scars of pain,
They remind me of freedom that I somehow regain

I gradually found peace and contentment in simplicity,
Leaving behind thorns and embracing serenity

10. Echo of Regret

Day and night ,there is echo of regret,
From silent corner of the room, which is hard to forget

As the autumn leaves part from tree with sorrow,
No wealth in the world can regain peace, tomorrow

Photos which are now faded and worn ,from past,
Remind me that life is transient, nothing will last

My singing in mountains would charm so strong,
Parting from hills is hard ,roots you belong

In the haste of chase, look what you lost,
No peace, no Joy, regrets fill my heart at its cost

Day and night there is echo of regret,
From the silent corners of room which is hard to forget

11. Heaven's Many Faces

For some, heaven is two square meals in a day,
For others, wealth and shine is less, which is their way

For some, heaven is a place where God resides,
For others ,it is about pleasures which world provides

They say money can buy happiness with its might,
Heaven is what you enjoy on earth and its savory delight

For some, heaven is in happiness of a child,
The shining bright eyes and the needs so mild

For others, Heaven could be a a life so free,
With a sense of wonder for nature and its trees

For me, heaven lies in our heart deep within
A sense of purpose ,a life to proclaim

12. Daughter of my heart

My daughter is my home, wonder of peace, where I
reside,
I see no were else happiness dwells ,with all its pride

You are like a gentle breeze and your laughter soothes
my soul,
When I think haywire ,your face reminds me of my goal

You are like a valentine rose with twinkle in your eyes,
May you get lots of power and reach new highs

You are chirruping in the house like a bird all the day,
Life may go up and down but you are my only way

You are my unshaken devotion that takes away all the
fear,
Wherever you go in world my blessings are with you my
sweetest dear

13. War Within

Many a times it comes in my mind,
Whether to go or wait till things unwind

Echoes of dilemma perplexes me again and again,
And I weigh the options but search still sustains

A field of battle, labyrinth of my own thought,
Confusions are bound to sustain of scars that lesson
taught

The path is unclear and the fate is stern,
How to move ahead with memories that I yearn

Many a times it comes in my mind,
Whether to go on wait till things unwind

14. Silent Reflections

15

Silence like snowflakes, beautifies everything with
serenity,
In the stillness of mind, you can find true clarity

Silence is as sparkling and glorious as gold,
Every situation unfolds, in the way you mould,

Silence is like a twilight, with some mystery,
Don't express to much, else it becomes history

Silence is answer to everything insane,
With arguments you gain nothing, except pain

Silence is the answer to everything done with heart,
Stillness of mind and composure is a marvelous art

15. Way to will

What is left when you weaken your will,
Live full of challenges has its own thrill

A life without obstacle or a test,
Is a life which cannot be led at its best

Unshaken and unturned is will like a stone,
Don't give up on challenges which are your own

When the phoenix rises from ashes to reborn,
Don't give up now for there is nothing to mourn

Will is what visionaries see for the dream,
So whimsical in every thought of its stream

So strong is the will which shows you the way,
Illuminating the path with happiness and gay

Whatever be the situation let your soul be your guide,
A source of strength and power deep inside

16. Embracing The Horizon

Life is beautiful to be enjoyed everyday,
Uncertainty is fearful ,but being positive is only way

Embracing every moment will test our might,
Take one step for journey of thousand miles ,with all the pride

No regret of past or worry of future, only commencing way,
Embracing the unknown is essence of life, yesterday and today

Dance to the mystery of life as the it unfolds,
Release yourself from everything that you left behind as old

The autumn leaves will wither and fall to the ground,
Pack your bags to explore the nature which has beauty unbound

17. Self- Assurance

Truth is a giant tree which stands tall,
Unshaken by wind of fancy which disguises all

It has its roots so deep and trunk so strong,
You can escape for a while but accept where you belong

You can run and hide but the truth will always find,
It's path has no regret where there is union of heart and mind

Truth will guide you the way in the darkest night,
A glorious beam that illuminates you with its light

It doesn't have to shout ,it's voice is always low,
It needs not praise itself ,it has its own glow

18. Grains of Sand

Happiness comes from little things of joy,
World is an orchestra of love, listen my boy!

Each moment is a Symphony, each breath is a rhyme,
Live every moment with gratitude, for we have little
time

True happiness is the tapestry of nature around,
Look !Pine trees have beauty unbound

Feed the hungry child and see sparkle in his eyes,
Give this world some love and see your happiness to rise

Don't slip away happiness like gains of sand,
For today is only promised that's only in our hand

19. A Mother's Legacy

My dear daughter what I give you is legacy of love,
May peace prevail with you my little dove

A legacy of freedom where you decide with glee,
Choices you make will be supported by me

The path you choose will always be your own,
Here I assure my heart is always your home

A legacy to embrace uncertainty and accept,
Wisdom to push away negativity and reflect

Go ahead with your priorities, rest doesn't matter,
People are double faced and their opinions scatter

I'll cheer your success and pacify your fears,
For you are more than life to me, my daughter dear

20. Self - Discovery

In my path of solitude, I take my flight,
A journey of self renewal without any plight

The stillness of solitude brightens my soul,
Observe the nature and the world as a whole

When the restless mind is harmed by complexity of
world,
It's the time to go closer to nature and stay uncurled

In solitude, you find answers that give you a rebirth,
To take next step and find the way of mirth

The melancholy given by the fake people will be washed
 with rain,
Learn to seclude yourself to get away from pain

21. Heart of the matter

In the heart of the matter ,we find the voice,
The decision to make, a matter of choice

Heart of the matter unravels what is true,
When you are lost in chaos and have no clue

Heart of the matter in life is love,
Unshaken, rooted and have strength above

When people try to demean you and say untrue,
With purity of heart, you find the clue

The envy of people will malice you with lies,
But you keep your heart pure for a heavenly surprise

Prayer to god will show you the light,
No matter how difficult, you embrace what is right

www.ingramcontent.com/pod-product-compliance
Lightning Source LLC
Chambersburg PA
CBHW071244140726
47996CB00007B/2741